This book belongs to:

_____

My Incredible Blankie

Marie Hinkle

Illustrated by
Gabby Correia

5 Sail Publishing
Jacksonville, Florida

Copyright © 2022 by Marie Hinkle

All rights reserved. No part of this book may be reproduced, stored in a retrieval system, or transmitted in any form or by any means, electronic, mechanical, photocopying, recording, or otherwise, without written permission from the publisher, 5 Sail Publishing, 14286 Beach Blvd., Ste. 19-277, Jacksonville, FL 32250, or through the publisher's website, www.5sailpublishing.com.

Book and cover design by 5 Sail Publishing and Sagaponack Books & Design

ISBNs:
978-1-7341248-6-6 (softcover)
978-1-7341248-7-3 (hardcover)
978-1-7341248-8-0 (e-book)

Library of Congress Control Number: 2022914142

Summary: A young boy who loves his blankie and takes it everywhere with him becomes upset when he discovers it missing, in the washing machine, and then the dryer.

JUV039050 Juvenile Fiction / Social Themes / Emotions & Feelings
JUV009050 Juvenile Fiction / Concepts / Senses & Sensation
JUV051000 Juvenile Fiction / Imagination & Play
JUV019000 Juvenile Fiction / Humorous Stories
JUV039090 Juvenile Fiction / Social Themes / New Experience

5 Sail Publishing
Jacksonville, Florida

Printed and bound in the United States of America
First Edition

This book is dedicated to my family and, more specifically, to my children. They have loved their blankies and have also inspired me to write their stories of adventure. It has been a pleasure to watch them learn and love while growing up with their blankies.

I am not sure where it came from, but it has always been here. From the moment I could breathe I felt its power. It has been here to comfort and support me every day.

It is a small square with a silky edge. It is strong and mighty like an ox, and yet, it is made with the softest fabric.

I love to smell it. I put my nose to my blankie and take a big whiff. ... The scent calms me. Whenever I feel sad, I bury my face into my blankie and I instantly feel better. It is soft and feels good rubbed against my face and then down my cheeks.

When I go to sleep, I need my blankie right next to me. At night we revisit our daring adventures from the day.

My blankie and I have made beady-eyed dogs back off. We took control of the scary potty. And we fanned away ferocious dust bunnies. There is nothing we cannot accomplish together—as a team.

When I wake up in the morning, the first thing I need is my blankie. I grab it to make sure it is safe and ready to start our day. We will be ready for anything. A huge smile stretches across my face.

One day I was playing with my train set. I began to get frustrated because the pieces were not fitting together. I went to my room to get my blankie, and it was gone! I panicked!

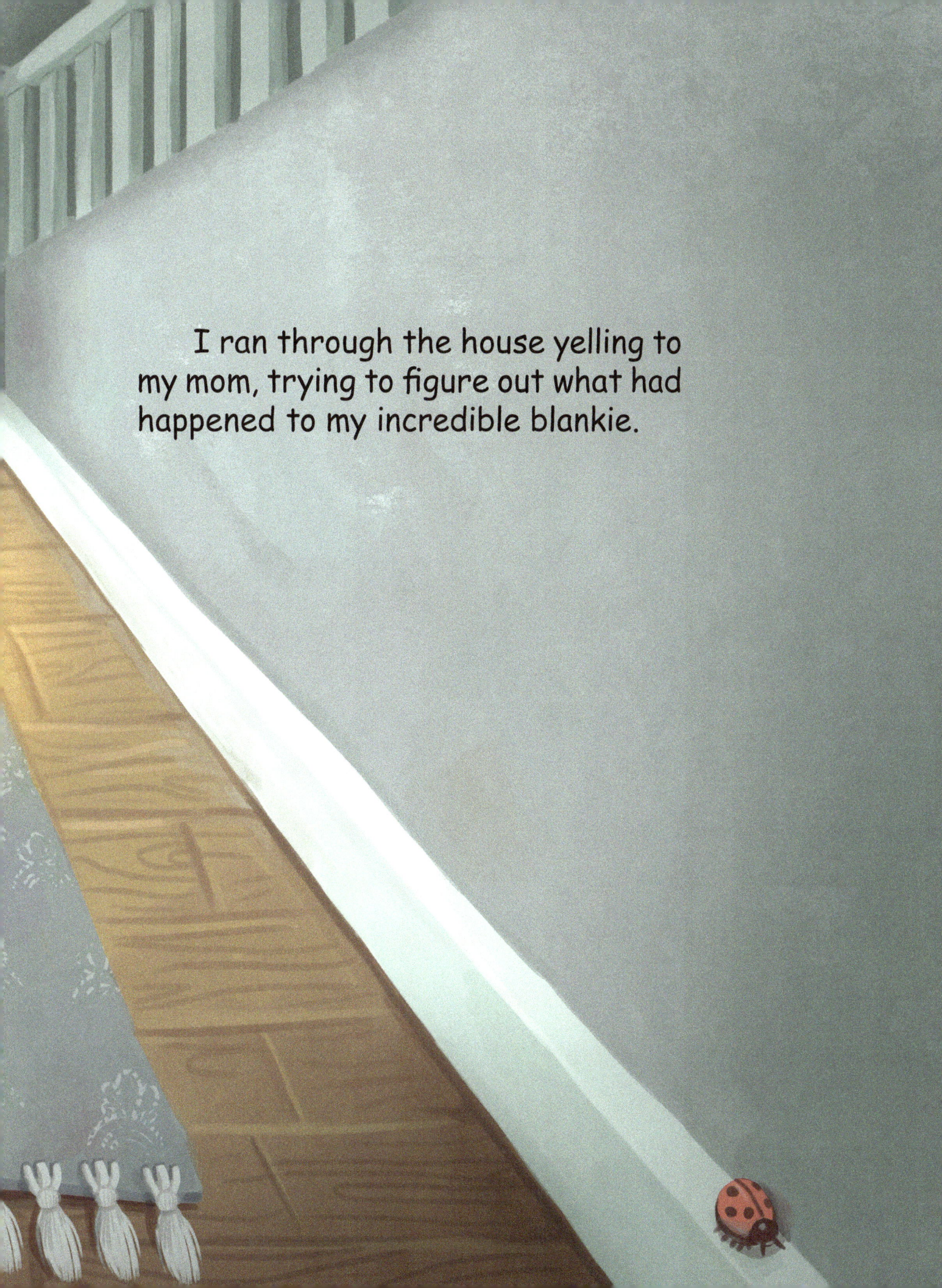

I ran through the house yelling to my mom, trying to figure out what had happened to my incredible blankie.

She told me it was taking a bath in the washing machine. She reached for my hand and walked me to the laundry room.

Mom showed me the humongous and loud washing machine, and I watched my poor blankie spinning, swishing, and rolling around in bubbles. I could see that my blankie was screaming and it wanted to be out, safe with me.

I turned to my mother and began to scream, cry, and throw the biggest fit I could. I now needed my blankie more than ever. I continued to watch it spin and, fortunately, the washer finally stopped. ... But it didn't end there. My mother put my wet blankie into another gigantic machine. She told me it was going to dry my blankie and that I would have it very soon.

I threw myself onto the floor, kicking and screaming. I was sobbing. I cried so hard, tears ran down my face while snot dripped from my nose. I wanted my blankie, and my blankie wanted me. Sadly, no one was listening.

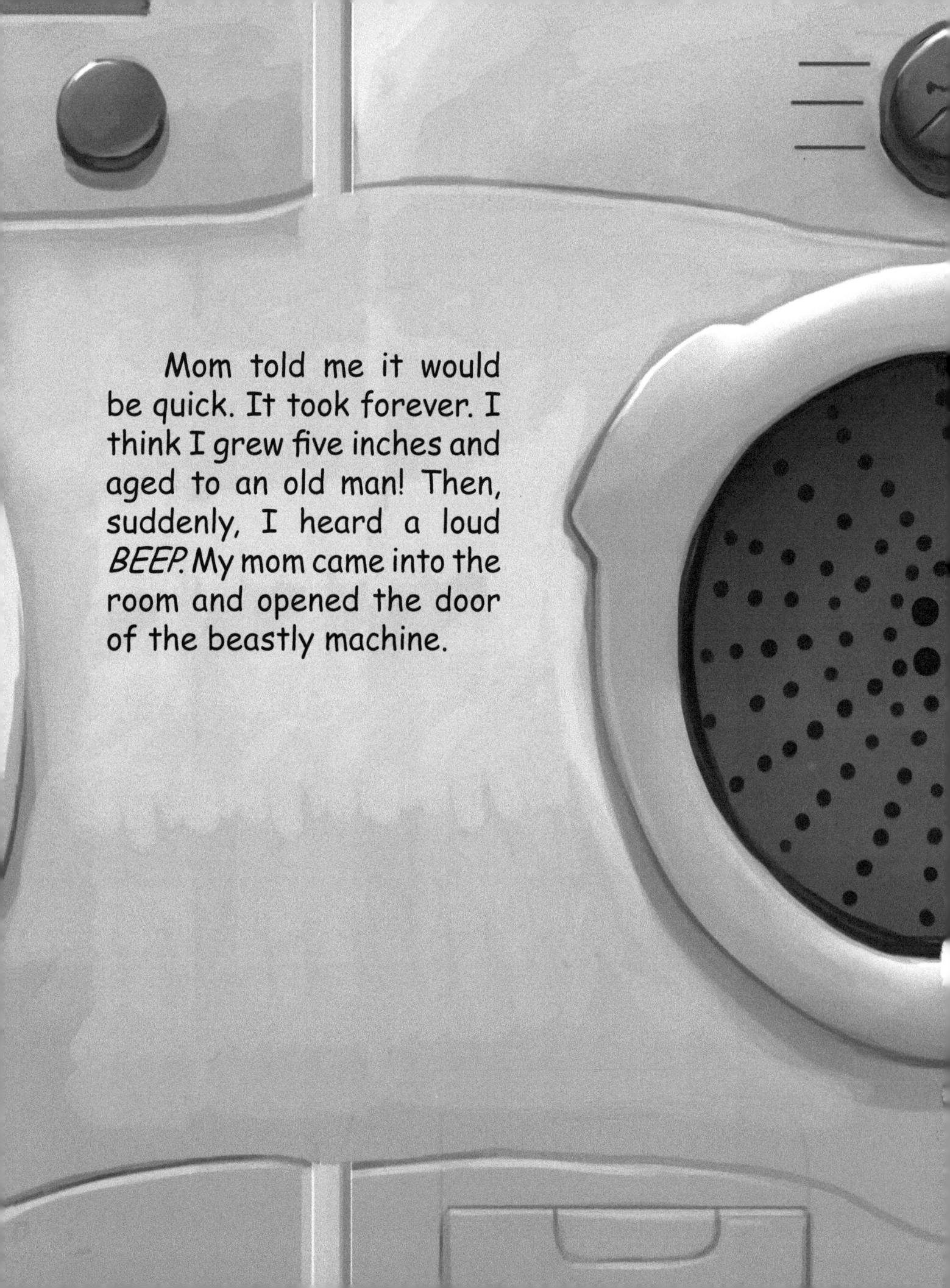

Mom told me it would be quick. It took forever. I think I grew five inches and aged to an old man! Then, suddenly, I heard a loud *BEEP.* My mom came into the room and opened the door of the beastly machine.

Something magical happened. My mother reached into the machine and pulled out my blankie. As soon as she handed it to me, I felt my heavy heartache disappear!

I rubbed the blankie over my face. I put my nose to my blankie to sniff the soothing scent. It smelled amazingly good. Rubbed on my swollen, wet, snotty cheeks, it felt silky smooth. In fact, my blankie felt and smelled better than ever! It was like new! My blankie was beyond happy as well, to not have chocolate, orange juice, and milk smeared all over it.

I picked up my blankie and ran as far away as I could from those scary machines and my mother. I went into my room, where I could be alone with my incredible blankie. I closed the door so we could have a private meeting about how we were going to make that train set work.

Activities

1. What insect can you see represented in the book?

2. How many times do you see this insect in the book?

3. Why do you think this insect is represented in this book?

4. Can you name or find five facts about this insect?

5. What do you think this insect and the main character in the book have in common?

6. Can you draw and label a picture of the insect?

7. On a separate piece of paper, draw a picture of something that is special to you. Make sure to include specific details: colors, patterns, texture, and size. Then create a background. Be creative. Share your picture with someone.

Discussion Questions

1. Do you have a favorite or special toy?

2. What is it?

3. Why is it your favorite?

4. Have you ever lost or misplaced your favorite toy?

5. What happened? Write or tell a story of how you lost and found your toy.

6. Do you sleep with your favorite toy?

7. Has your special toy ever gotten dirty? Write or tell how your favorite toy got dirty.

8. Have you ever gotten frustrated?

9. What were you frustrated about and how did you solve your problem?

10. What advice can you give to others on how to handle frustration?

ABOUT THE AUTHOR

Marie Hinkle is a seasoned educator who has had the opportunity to teach in several schools across the United States. This is her third published children's book. Mrs. Hinkle is passionate about reading and empowering children. She lives in Florida with her husband and three children. Her family continues to inspire her to write books. In her free time, she loves to travel and spend time with her family at the beach.

Learn more about Marie at:
5sailpublishing.com.

ABOUT THE ILLUSTRATOR

Gabby Correia (NightshadeBerry) is a digital artist, illustrator, and portrait artist. She has been working as a digital artist and illustrator for about ten years. Her passion is illustrating children's books and stories for independent authors. In her spare time, she enjoys reading, hiking, and spending time with loved ones.

www.ingramcontent.com/pod-product-compliance
Lightning Source LLC
Chambersburg PA
CBHW061114070526
44583CB00027B/3290